QUENCH

QUENCH

Poems by Amy Orazio

CW Books

Published by CW Books
P.O. Box 541106
Cincinnati, OH 45254-1106

ISBN: 9781625492647

Poetry Editor: Kevin Walzer
Business Editor: Lori Jareo

Visit us on the web at www.readcwbooks.com

Dedication

This book is for Mark Neilson, who taught me to be wild
and taught me to be home.

Acknowledgements

It is with gratitude that I acknowledge that variations of these poems first appeared in: *Bitterzoet, Chaparral, Cobalt Review, Dream Fever Magazine, Gap Tooth, H_N_GM_N, Pidgeonholes, The Curator, Ruminate Magazine, Synaesthesia,* and *Timber Journal.*

Table of Contents

HARBOR

HEADWATER

Stone Would Be Water

Stone would be water

But it cannot undo

Its own hardness

Rocks might run

Wild as torrents

Plunged upon the sky

By cliffs none climb

Who makes fountains

Spring from flint

Who dares tell

One thirsting

There's a well

-Samuel Menashe, *Eyes Open to Praise*

DESERT

Exit Scene

Where the amber sings to dark
darkness rings
a gradient crest
rolling line of red gold
fire-scoured stones
spilling water
singing us next
when you see it don't keep moving
set up camp set
by this light
examine milk teeth
pull the soft one
to six hundred deep
our gradient call
thick to thin
in turmoil to relief
dance here desert
night of rolling feet
gradient acoustics
a swollen to receded sea

Slake

We wake

spread stateless

before morning

the dark is a teller

but won't atone

like water

this season's knotted earth

will crackle

your throat knows

what it wants

to say to you

By This I Mean

A place where the sky

holds its breath

and the snake extracts water

from its prey

arid womb as an altar

stones do right

before seeing, asking

help and what

are you thirsty for?

Faults Are Present

This present basin
whose floor is marked
with low ridges
and the plate
that moves wreath-like

How fingers meet
how bones in the hands
are loose they rattle
and the earth's sediment forms
magnets in green-violet ears
hover where north and east
are unzipped as a ribcage
pulled from nights like these
the plate is hot
and eroding borders

How words get inside
slippery
forming as faces

orange garnets to swallow
summer-lit bruising to God
to the I and the am

What is Left

Olive salt
in your fingerprint
to lick the center
I have been waiting for
this raven gift

You say I am
cavernous
it is
but all of the stones
have not been
dismissed

Hull me
I have touched
every edge of the creek
what is left is
Elijah skin

Kindling

Milkweeds spring

from the soil

parched mouths graze

a fire is set

like that

Here and in a wet climate

plants grow back

one fall

they'll brush my knee

wild for now

I carry your seed

Early Ash

We read a medical book

an excuse to sit close

in tight text

marrow lives

in the cavity of bones

at birth it's all red

Strange to turn pages

with you the terms blur

our evening air thick

after summer's wildfire

foreheads smudge, looking

Forward to late winter

when Good Friday snaps

and opening is feeling

old pages under thumbs

the ground is smoldering still

Miracle

"Yes how can I answer your question please?"

A crow spins around the room. Eyes pass through me like water.

My hand wilts, released.

"I read Exodus by George Oppen. So I was hoping to see."

Further In

When taste buds meet tongue

lapping is sewing

bumps to run fingers on

wanting for milk

gold as the honey thread

here our hereditary bones

are one:

firewood

to pile or pull from

the thread of this kiss

(we hang on to)

the sweet burnt texture

of those who come for the son

Past the Brook

Those buried sources go
west of west
to gather commodities
lubricant for throat
crow's caw hangs
honey-er than thick
a flag half-mast
evidence slipped

The widow has her own song
she is setting supper
but her bread is gone
can you pray for oil?

I need oil to pray
to unearth these desert tricks

Red-Bone Walk

And red-bone crouch
the desert foams
toward a song
searching for a well
with scrubland mothers
that shed and trill

To sing the city by night
is sticky as skin
but what skin is good
in rattlesnake country?
all hollowed
those words off the canyon

Gauze

I dream to them

steam fills the room

God at the window

says, "Exit again"

Veil

A wild choice—

to suspend between two hours

liquid as a veil.

The feeling that comes when you can't remember if someone you know

is dead or alive.

Not the missing but the forgetting.

The slipping.

Was this a choice?

I blink and dusk is gone. Open my eyes

to the moment

right before the fire hits the match.

The problem isn't the hour I was born into, it's the hour I'm missing out

on. The problem is the thirst (I don't know how to learn to drink I just

have to drink).

The god who woke me up has many voices. They blend like water.

A choice

to feel the feeling

of being

swallowed up in a child's laughter.

Not the sound but the light of it.

Honeyed.

As it pours over me I hear it

has never been a problem

"The fire comes from the scratch"

Leaving

To find a love
as feral as

Or just a body
of water

CITY

Of Angels

Instead, a circle of light

imbedded

what carried me

to the aqueduct

for survival

masts of marrow

bright

I asked for this shroud

for this city in me

to be laid bare

At the Metro Station

Where dry is a reason
bone is a name meaning
miracles like tide pools
gather at our feet
as a home
for the remains
bent here the undead
lemon trees are ripe
from the waist
their witness
is reason enough to heal
or reason enough to stay

Is Thirsting Seeing

Below the bridge
at the Los Angeles River
mid-evening
red-tipped blackbirds
gather berries
to drop at our feet
for supper or confirmation
in dry heat
nothing-is-as-it-is
a fire in the bushel
some trash can
hiding is-it-this?
the new son sings

Backlit

A figure stands on Santa Monica's shore

between pier and sunset

the silhouette of a man:

six wings black against a sherbet sky

kaleidoscope here

for the sense of passage

or the gathering

of salt fish

Incarnate

Whose teeth

and whose thumbnails and thighs

blood curtain

whose priest

bones grind the monument

on 5th and Olive

petrified fish by the basin

stay for a three-layered supper

a dry wine to sprinkle

whose sweat

swells back to life

Transfigure

At a switchback on Topanga Canyon

white inside white

smell from the foot on snakehead ascent

will you braid my hair

when you feel your fingers again?

snake coiling at my back

primrose and thyme

bursting into flames into white

ligament by ligament climb

spinning the rotary

fevered then he

in white

with the dead

but alive but dead as three

layered back and forward

raised as water

white can see

As Strangers

On Venice Beach a baseball cap man nearby
I speak in tongues he asks if I want weed or what?
a shorebird flies out of my mouth it rolls beside us
ferris wheel to the north but his laugh is a foam
response: it's not too polluted here to swim or for barbeques?
and finally words not legal but great for taking pictures

Sink

Though our bodies can lapse

we still have to eat

to set a table

with a bruised pear

lost

at the bottom of the bowl

what does it mean

when the sun sinks low

bruising the sky

beautiful

can be a troubling word

I still believe in it though

like angels

who wear faces

bodies that forget fast

traffic is a whirling dervish

tire tongues

stick fallen fruit to a basin

lid at 5 pm

it hums and spits

and beats like wings

we still have to eat

The City Of Angels

can be troubling

a name we feel in our mouth:

hard to use

or hard to be found

Subtropical

Extinguished
by a silver ribbon
that slices the state in half
through canyon and desert
to the jacarandas
who unfist petals
flush streets
leaving limbs naked
to see light through
a milky dusk
we stay put
locked in valley bodies
that float the aqueduct
watering us still
unwatering enough

Drained

Bath water
pooled in a navel
the only drink left

Sabbath

Sunday's head is heavy
already leathering
palm trees curl north
all of our daughters
wear visors lately
skip lunch
hang jasmine
around their neck
I see water stains
in a drought
blondewood pews
pull us in from the sun
we dream of
the sacrament
hungry and
the wet slaughter
of Noah's flood

Nimble

To open two hands
and barter for a fig sapling
is wanting for a body
the feel of California
sagebrush against bare
seed in a ravine
will sprawl without water
here the soil shouldn't womb
yarrows and trees
but here we give in to it
lean to it
brash to say I need skin
to split anyway

Wait Here

In that a wolf prowl

lands north before it laps

October's cadence

senses my eyes

in the dark

but not dark enough

in that an Indian summer

sears a latitude

whose tongue

a cartographer

of the San Gabriel Mountains

in that the pines hold

sienna the smell

of careless birdhands

me disparate trails

wait here but don't waste

here like them the difference

in that flaw my country

my flag is near

Reach

Penny behind my teeth

token from the desert

when I say longing

he asks for the word

wanting

some coppery taste

let me see your lips chapped

and marbled by the sea

the six o'clock wind

transposes him

from under to in

finder to found

language beckons again

hook your finger here

no sea where I am

spilling forward wishing

is the same as wanting

here is becoming

sticky as sound

Dead for the Eating

Pheasants

around your neck

iridescent feathers

wave hello

this is foreign land

my mouth is dry

and colorless

I need an archer

in the cottonwood cooing

What I Forbore

When you call I hear the desert
and the place right after
when I respond
a mouth full of bees
"The Pacific wasn't enough"
isn't a question
if a town wasn't inside of you
marching if I didn't need
to ascend a sound
I haven't broken
the habit of prayer
I'm still asking questions
I'm due farther
north than the hive can reach

HARBOR

Cargo

Her is their
California sea-thighs
time is the skin of the desert
"I scatter"
"I spread about"
"between, through, across"
however many she is
depends on the hour
but this is a work about the body
sailing
for a host country

Reservoir

The excavation

made room for bidding

for voices warm

under my tongue

the bird of thirst mimics hunger

a call to find and oil the door

at dusk while the basin is wet

Yell Smoke

On an amberstill night
to pour is to strike death
clapped in the ribs
whose end the rhythm
trailing a grass fire
from city to harbor
slippery feet
salted as walls
clap too are
muskroot flowers
crushed and distilled
carried in a censer
to burn the atonement
to burn for the exile's well

Pulled

From a damp pocket
the hawk who found the bud
or was it you peering up?
that night you came wintered
time stamped us fresh
the east wind hollowed
you were a cavity
ghosted in the trees
quiet like the harbor-side
our moon undone

Rinse

Is this the house
of breaking water
of learning how limbs hum
with the current
three always present
hovering here
knotted from the plunge

Birdchorus

Swallows, a witness to truth:

the bramble of you

native region

tangled

the doe of you

eyes a frozen country

spare limbs crossed

the complex tart of you

tobacco forest

thick

a birdchorus watched

my temperature lost

the home of what I knew

Remain

There is a jar where I keep the sea
when it shuts off its sounds
where the callous of noon is trimmed
with radishes, olive boughs
behind my headboard
I whisper with the cartographer
pointed north to a broken wind

We are the bramble
he tells me
untangle fingers
and find a grey light
to bury in

Terminal

The heat of hummingbirds in our throats

a thousand morning wings

beating into

this tense landing strip

here the pulling of the tide

here we are caught

in the density of

an aggravated

harvested crop

Suckledry

The one about my love for you

as spring follows a ripe wind

that hums and batters

the skin of a peach

in due time your limbs tender

November's chill

will carry them south

stretched pink but ours

affixed to us

Breakwater

Or how I lost you
when I listened
to a cistern
current of she who
was left our bodies
fall easier
this time of year

Knot-Tied

Listen—

the hiss and roil

this time walk the soil under

the distance from mother to daughter

firmament to earth

like dye seeping through

footfalls that hold

what she left

the red berry of her

rattle sings

drowsy in her skin

she would tell you to rest

HEADWATER

Thin Places

C-shaped section of a river

for bending

or laying

when loss

makes room for

what happens at the water's side

Unhinge

Although there is
the voice the night makes
the sound of one world
halving from another
the ladder remains
creamy light this place
to spread out
swollen on the delta
where did you go
in the throat of the cedarwaxwing
where there is no west to be fed
there is the shedding skin
copper flakes at the water's edge
to let the earth seep through
fix your fingers to my mouth
to be found again

In Between

Wanting the weight

of drowning

of your hand pinned on my chest

The stars are drowning too

a deep hum at midnight

thick on our tongues:

the language of your hand

is the in between heavy

cloud cover murmuring

How good does it feel

to unsee

Shelter

The bear carcass inside of you
I crawl in
all of these frames you provide
cleaned salmon bones
to hold my hair in place
the silt lifted
your shoulder blades
posts at the river bank

There You Are

A study in empty as broken
stones as altars yield
a harbor to tell
now that I can drink
I know what's refracting
the door that's open
I know what I'm thirsty for

Revelate

A half-moon portal
unfanned before us
the holy soil cradles
evenings who lift their heads
with birch wires that praise:
the clack-whirr and still of
backlit spindles
your forearms holding the rain
the smell of being soaked
dried and soaked again
crushed into river bone
rocks in the cove sing heavy
splendored until they unpeel into
text, crystals that
anchor us back
holding
like your wet hand
crescents in the canoe

Open Wide

Depth into depth
into a cortex to touch
the handprints inside of us
the handprints on the door leading out
winter's men turn in
to ash like the tissue of manna
the manna is another door
to feel for
the call of bells breaking in
a voice like snow
white of the raven's crust

Seraphim

Burnished song
at the island
threshold of and to

and two and two and two
wings
can you see?

Tapestry grows from the head: he
(one by one by one)
swallows
corners: bird men sing
on invisible wires

isle of heat
I might die downwind of
mowing wings

subdivision
thrush these

six branch firs
holding tongs for my

tongue
washed in a fire
swallow this moon!

wings:
a gushing spring surrounding who
ascended
a sending

I was a far off tree called in
nobody saw the port that I entered in and
nothing appeared to

Of Many Waters

Language at the thunderhead

like pausing or washing

how it feels to be found

crackling after a fever

the sky sounding out words

lung-thin

and getting thinner

by the hour

Shroud

I name my body
according to proximity
but in an almost wilderness
skin can only guess wet
based on the walls around my breath
based on the walls of pines
fracturing light
through clasped fingers
is to see in part
is to know in part
the names for tree needles
curled in thirst for faith
that comes like this
nameless as faceless
shadows across landscapes

Fine Printed Spines

The question is sectional

it's a mountain range of

is there such a thing

as a tree that rose from the dead

how under the root

emerald in motion

at the volition of who

bolsters light that pulls up and through

what stands to canopy

a thicket

where is it rivering to

Water to Live Water to Die

Except that—

this is not a metaphysical choice

this is gut

'and out of your bellies shall flow

rivers of living water'

this is about the body

body holds spirit here

sings the unserious

blood

Darkened Not Completely Dark

for John Taggart

If we could hear the voice

would it matter

or know the naming of the names

gathered tight then unfurled

like snow between pines

here ground here fowl here fish

and here vault what a sky

brooding it's enough

to watch the clouds clap and boil

to see the skin of the river wrinkle

or the feathers on the wrens

lift and fall

to hear the whirr of the wind chase

after days ice cold and stealing branches

to eat oranges for breakfast

and rub sage brush

into ashes or resin

between palms

sticky the root

of the berry bush

is a murmur

under soil formed then reformed

to know or dig after

the sound is something

but to feel

the spirit hovering

before calling like light

is the bell is the light

Unscathed

Then I was watered

as the night sucked the gold out of the air

as I danced and desert spilled from my feet

as the trees shed their skin

like snakes

Then I wore your skin

face framing my face

as the sea rushed in

to border me again

honey colored

words were stuck

at the back of my throat

As the moon

flickered its light

tongue on wave crests

surrendered to break

Meaning the night was good

and the time just after that was

When I saw the city

glimmering hive of bees

to kiss my lovers was

to scratch and sting

The bedrock of a mouth

but even then

troubling as

Crumbling soil

felt ash-kneed

I could sing to the next

as your blood-song

pulsed me west

wombed and underneath

Where trees wear your skin

haloed in fog

this word that dips deep

in the headwater

to drink is to see

to be blanketed

watered again

Boundary

Following lines that fall soft
startle at first
in the dark fingers over eyes
start to surface
spring before I feel shape
at the river's edge
the flood recedes
the herons don't mind
they are watching too drawing
and waiting the minnows flap so
drastic a sound hollowed
out praise for a place
made in winter
for proceeds from the east
until the current switched
fork spooled winds
deep like the lines
they wing-beat
then lay pleasant
and broad so western
to leave room my limbs

held out like cups

for this year's portion

To Be Under and In

Fingers of angels who look like men

on a skyline of blue firs

to be sent

through a portal

to whirl like them

in love or fall

stuck

burnished by seraphim

who look like all

eyes on eyes on eyes

to see jasper is

to be cupped

by the earth at the trunk

to be sung under northern lights

Hover

Here where we share the morning fog
over the water
where water is a mountain and it is selected
where the soft mountain of
your body holds the hum of
headwaters north
two bodies of water
curling into one
spilling over state lines
here where we are soft with lines
as they fold north to south to west
the coordinates of the moon
bowing as yesterday
here the borders selected as water
are soft as we trace
holy as we return

Canal

Interlaced

from our window

outlining the ghost

of where we've been

the ghost behind

our tongue lives

vibrating

this is our drink

from a copper kettle river

the rise-and-fall

warmstill as we are

unfinished

our green center womb

translucent

in the trembling

This is About You and I

When we were kinned

inside or outside our bodies

when we forgot how to hold our bodies

when we were still for fear

of a break when we were thin-spindly

strangling too full

sap heavy limbs

we were folded home from fringes

sea city desert

crumbled we were

needled into soil

pulled and wet-forwarded

summitted up

Ripening

We opened our eyes

where timber once stood

in the citrus light of the spring

someone said

what kind of hawk in us

our mouths stitched together

saltlicked we're cathedrals here

when the soil unfolds

broadwinged

water is the prayer

ready enough to be sung

Gratitude

I couldn't have created this book without the following supporters and inspirers: Caleb Orazio (lover), Rachel McLeod Kaminer, Sierra Nicole Qualles and Rocio Carlos (poets), Paul Vangelisti, Dennis Phillips and Danell Bemis (teachers), and Kayla Lance and Sarah Warren (cover artists).

Printed in Great Britain
by Amazon

33381127R00061